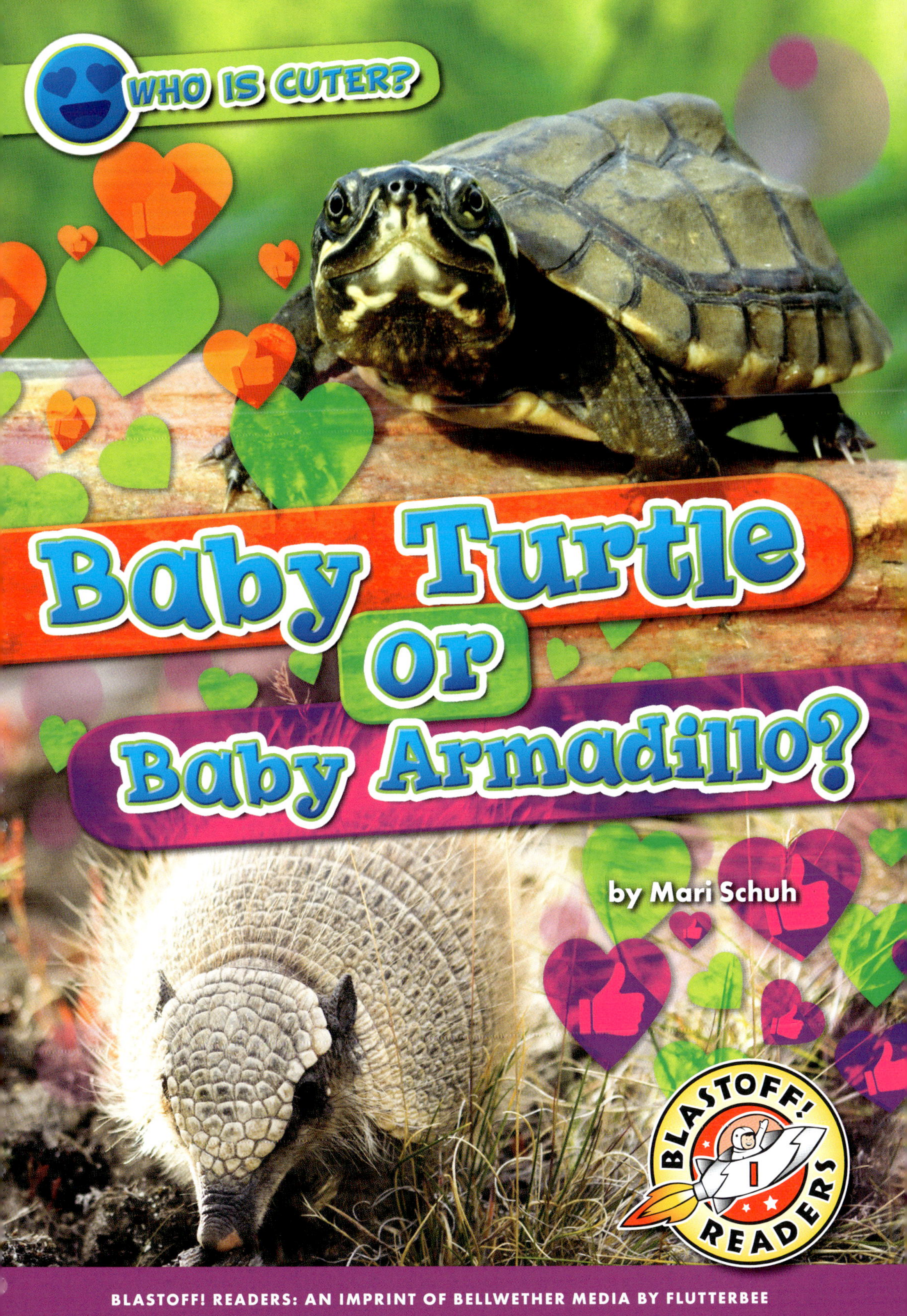

BLASTOFF! READERS: AN IMPRINT OF BELLWETHER MEDIA BY FLUTTERBEE

Blastoff! Readers are carefully developed by literacy experts to build reading stamina and move students toward fluency by combining standards-based content with developmentally appropriate text.

Level 1 provides the most support through repetition of high-frequency words, light text, predictable sentence patterns, and strong visual support.

Level 2 offers early readers a bit more challenge through varied sentences, increased text load, and text-supportive special features.

Level 3 advances early-fluent readers toward fluency through increased text load, less reliance on photos, advancing concepts, longer sentences, and more complex special features.

★ **Blastoff! Universe**

Reading Level

Grade K

Grades 1–3

Grade 4

This edition first published in 2026 by Bellwether Media, Inc.

For information regarding permission, write to Bellwether Media, Inc., Attention: Permissions Department, 3500 American Blvd W, Suite 150, Bloomington, MN 55431.

Library of Congress Cataloging-in-Publication Data is available at www.loc.gov or upon request from the publisher.

ISBN: 9798893047752 (hardcover)
ISBN: 9798893048759 (ebook)

Editor: Rachael Barnes

Printed in the United States of America, North Mankato, MN.

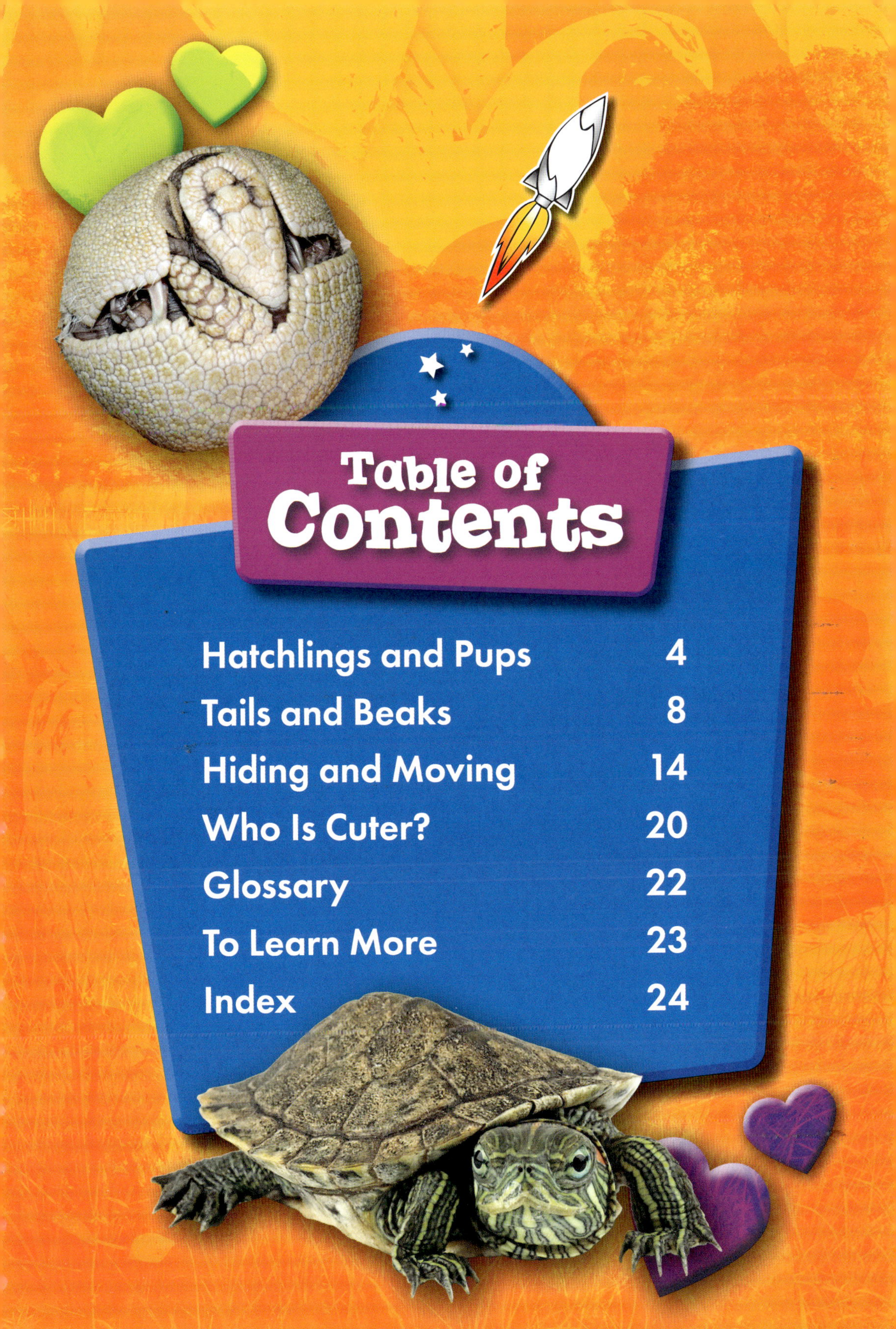

Table of Contents

Hatchlings and Pups 4
Tails and Beaks 8
Hiding and Moving 14
Who Is Cuter? 20
Glossary 22
To Learn More 23
Index 24

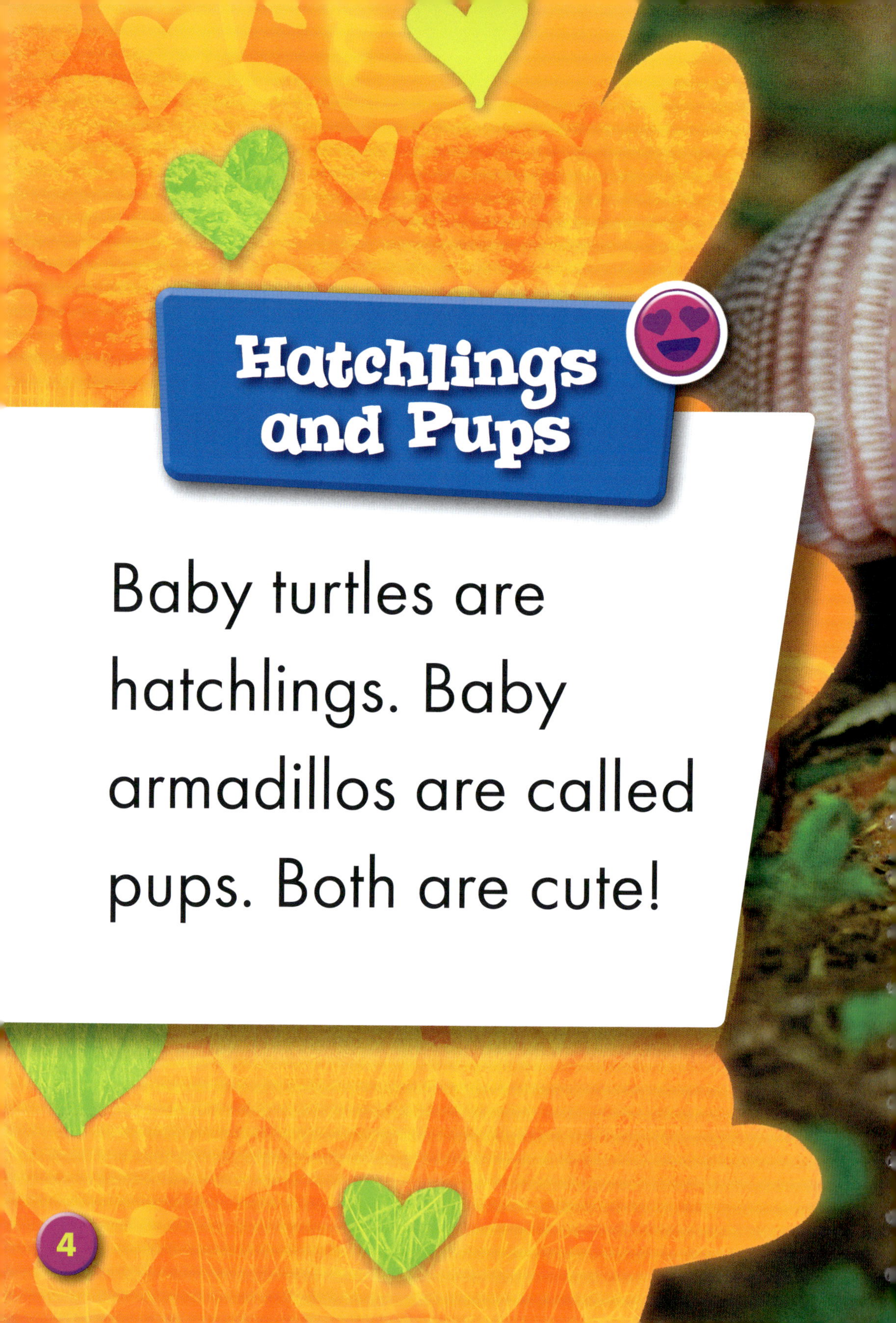

Hatchlings and Pups

Baby turtles are hatchlings. Baby armadillos are called pups. Both are cute!

pup
hatchling

Both babies have **shells**. Shells help keep them safe.

shell

Tails and Beaks

Hatchlings are **reptiles**. Pups are **mammals**.

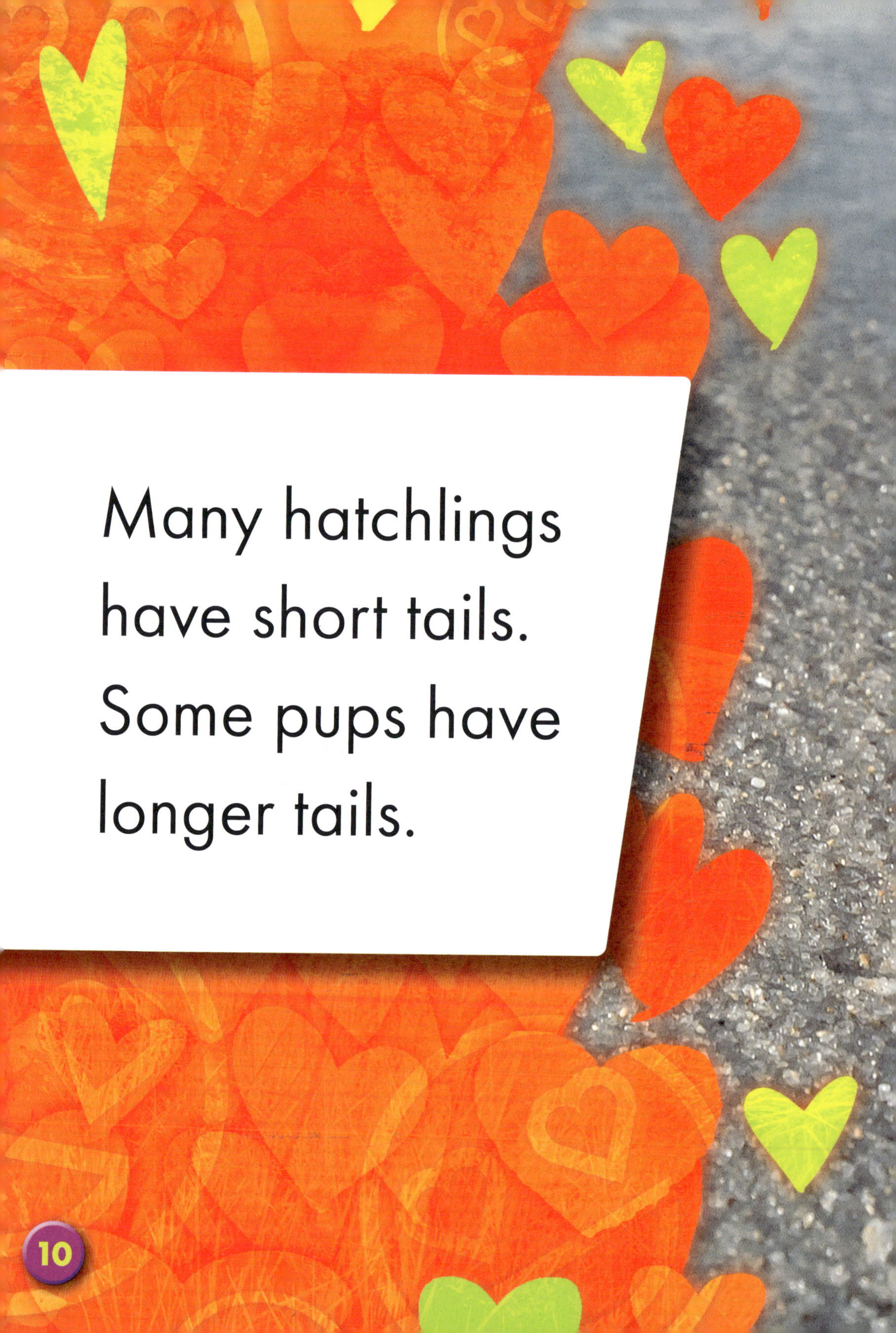

Many hatchlings have short tails. Some pups have longer tails.

longer tail
short tail

Hatchlings have **beaks**. They bite food. Older pups grab bugs with their sticky tongues.

beak
tongue

Hiding and Moving

Hatchlings live on their own. Pups grow up with mom.

mom

Most hatchlings can hide in their shells. Some pups roll into balls.

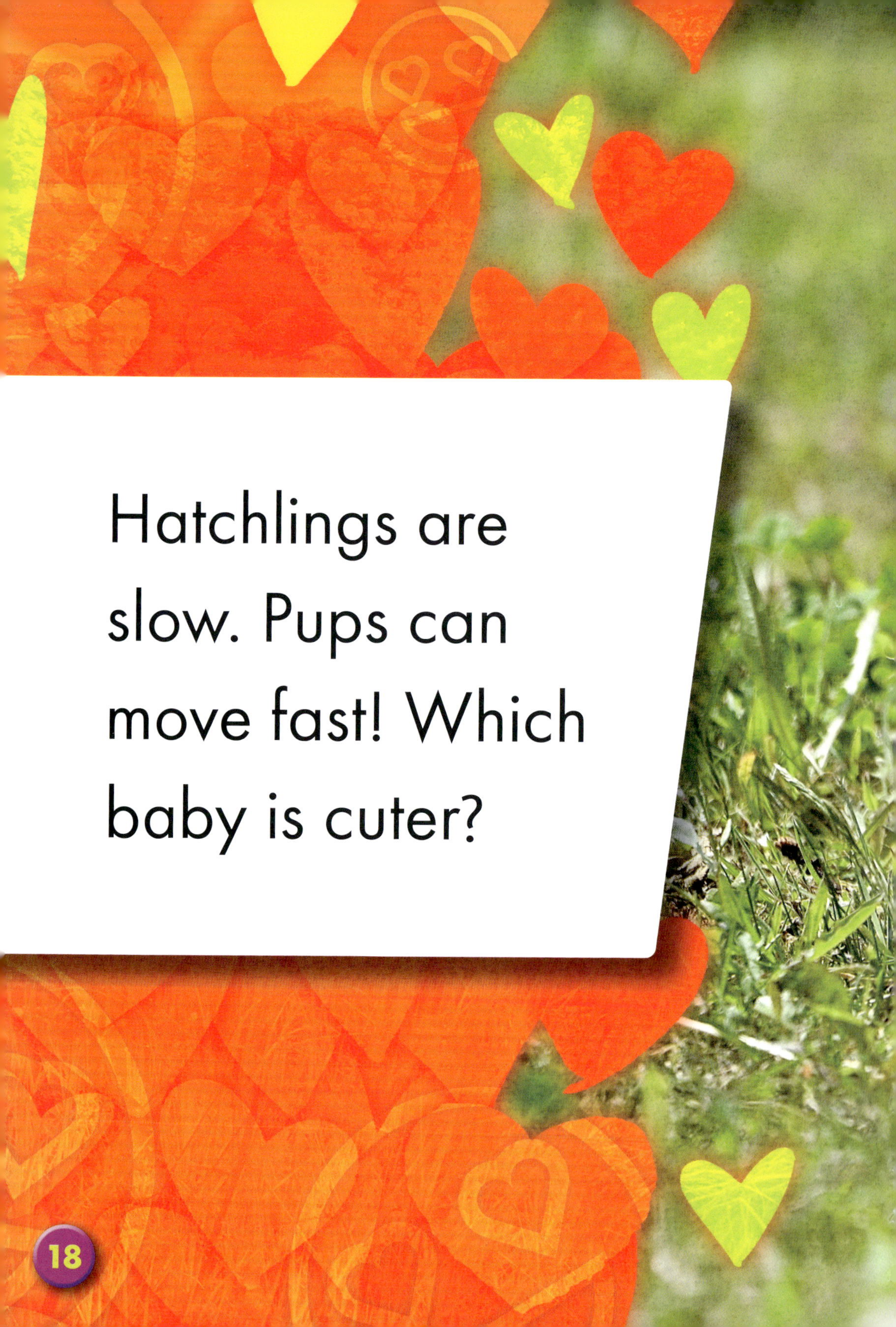

Hatchlings are slow. Pups can move fast! Which baby is cuter?

Who Is Cuter?

short tail

beak

Baby Turtle

lives on its own

hides in its shell

slow

Who is your pick?
Vote at
BellwetherMedia.com
sticky
tongue
longer tail
Baby Armadillo
grows
up with
mom
rolls into
a ball
fast

Glossary

beaks

the mouths of turtles

reptiles

cold-blooded animals that lay eggs

mammals

warm-blooded animals that have backbones and feed their young milk

shells

the hard coverings of some animals

To Learn More

AT THE LIBRARY

Riggs, Kate. *Armadillos.* Mankato, Minn.: Creative Education and Creative Paperbacks, 2023.

Ruby, Rex. *A Turtle Grows.* Bloomington, Minn.: Bearport Publishing, 2026.

Watt, E. Melanie. *Nine-banded Armadillo.* New York, N.Y.: Lightbox Learning Inc., 2025.

ON THE WEB

FACTSURFER

Factsurfer.com gives you a safe, fun way to find more information.

1. Go to www.factsurfer.com.
2. Enter "baby turtle or baby armadillo" into the search box and click 🔍.
3. Select your book cover to see a list of related content.

Index

armadillos, 4
beaks, 12, 13
bite, 12
hide, 16
mammals, 8
mom, 14, 15
reptiles, 8
roll, 16
shells, 6, 7, 16
speed, 18
tails, 10, 11
tongues, 12, 13
turtles, 4

The images in this book are reproduced through the courtesy of: Bran Photography, front cover (armadillo); AgriTech, front cover (turtle); Oksana178, front cover (background); Richard OD, background (throughout); belizar73, pp. 3 (armadillo), 17; Kurit atshen, p. 3 (turtle); Heidi and Hans-Juergen Koch/ Minden, pp. 4-5, 12-13; Pavel, pp. 5, 20 (slow); Andrew, pp. 6-7; Alizada Studios, p. 7; Rosanne Tackaberry/ Alamy Stock Photo, pp. 8-9; Karen Yomalli, p. 9; simoneemanphoto, pp. 10-11; Anadolu/ Contributor/ Getty Images, pp. 11, 14-15, 21 (grows up with mom); KCULP, pp. 13, 20 (lives on its own); Hunter, p. 15; Frost Photography/ Getty Images, pp. 16-17; helen Reid, pp. 18-19; Danielle Kiemel/ Getty Images, p. 19; Jenniveve84/ Getty Images, p. 20 (turtle); Frost, p. 20 (lives in shell); Josanel Sugasti, p. 21 (armadillo); belizar, p. 21 (rolls into ball); GUILLAUME SOUVANT/ Contributor/ Getty Images, p. 21 (fast); Hamilton, p. 22 (beaks); Andy Catlin/ 500px/ Getty Images, p. 22 (mammals); Subkhan08, p. 22 (reptiles); Takeapic4me, p. 22 (shells); alju, p. 22 (turtle).